DIVE IN!
KIDS'
BIBLE STUDY
NOTEBOOK

BARBOUR **kidz**
A Division of Barbour Publishing

Published by Barbour Publishing, Inc., 1810 Barbour Drive, Uhrichsville, Ohio 44683, www.barbourbooks.com

Our mission is to inspire the world with the life-changing message of the Bible.

Member of the
Evangelical Christian
Publishers Association

Printed in China.
000871   1021   DS

GO DEEP WITH GOD. . . BY STUDYING HIS WORD!

You have a natural enthusiasm and passion to learn, so here is a great tool to help you go deep with God. A follow-up to Barbour's *Dive In! Kids' Study Bible* and *Dive In! Devotions for Kids*, this study notebook provides space for you to capture insights from your own times in God's Word.

Each page includes simple prompts such as

- Who are your top 3 Bible characters? Why?

- What is your favorite Bible story? What's so special about it?

- Find an important verse to memorize, and write it here: _____. Now, memorize it!

Created especially for 8–12-year-olds, this notebook could be the beginning of a lifelong journey of discovery. You want to go deep with God—dive into His Word!

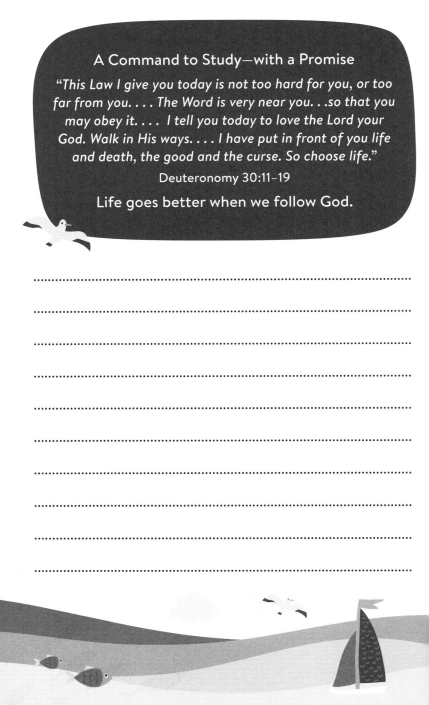

A Command to Study—with a Promise

"This Law I give you today is not too hard for you, or too far from you. . . . The Word is very near you. . .so that you may obey it. . . . I tell you today to love the Lord your God. Walk in His ways. . . . I have put in front of you life and death, the good and the curse. So choose life."

Deuteronomy 30:11–19

Life goes better when we follow God.

What is your favorite Bible story?
What's so special about it?

....

....

....

....

....

....

....

....

....

....

....

....

....

....

Imagine being able to talk to the author of a book you're reading. You could ask for help when something is confusing. . . and get "insider information" on the meaning and purpose of the book. With the Bible, you can always do that, since the Author is God Himself. And He is always willing to hear you, when you honestly and humbly pray for help in studying His Word.

Jot down a prayer for God's guidance as you study:

....

....

....

....

....

....

....

....

Who are your top 3 Bible characters?
Why?

....

....

....

....

....

....

....

....

....

....

....

....

....

....

Any time you study God's Word,
remember the five W and an H questions:
Who? What? When? Where? Why? How?
Read slowly, and really think
about what's there!

Which Bible character do you like most? Why?

....

....

....

....

....

....

....

....

....

....

....

....

....

Do you prefer to study your Bible in the morning, the middle of the day, or at night?

Make a plan for this week to spend time each day with God's Word.

....

....

....

....

....

....

....

....

....

....

....

....

....

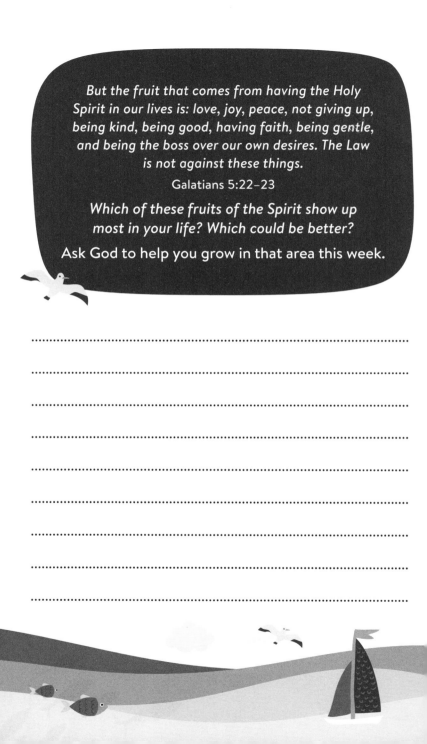

But the fruit that comes from having the Holy Spirit in our lives is: love, joy, peace, not giving up, being kind, being good, having faith, being gentle, and being the boss over our own desires. The Law is not against these things.

Galatians 5:22–23

Which of these fruits of the Spirit show up most in your life? Which could be better?

Ask God to help you grow in that area this week.

....

....

....

....

....

....

....

....

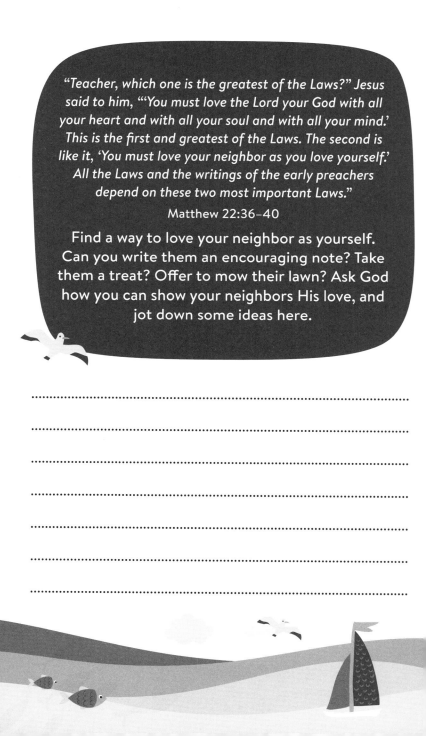

"*Teacher, which one is the greatest of the Laws?*" *Jesus said to him, "'You must love the Lord your God with all your heart and with all your soul and with all your mind.' This is the first and greatest of the Laws. The second is like it, 'You must love your neighbor as you love yourself.' All the Laws and the writings of the early preachers depend on these two most important Laws."*

Matthew 22:36–40

Find a way to love your neighbor as yourself. Can you write them an encouraging note? Take them a treat? Offer to mow their lawn? Ask God how you can show your neighbors His love, and jot down some ideas here.

....

....

....

....

....

....

....

Find three different verses that mention the word *life*. Write them here.

What can you learn from these verses?

....

....

....

....

....

....

....

....

....

....

....

....

....

Doodle a verse you love.
Make it creative by using colored pens
or pencils, stickers, paint, or markers!

....

....

....

....

....

....

....

....

....

....

....

....

....

....

Think of some tough thing you've dealt
with lately. Write it here, if you'd like.
Now, spend some time giving
this challenge to Jesus.

Give all your worries to Him because He cares for you.
1 Peter 5:7

....

....

....

....

....

....

....

....

....

....

For the Word of the Lord is right.
He is faithful in all He does.

Psalm 33:4

God promises to be faithful in all He does
and throughout all time. List some times when
you've seen His faithfulness in your own life.

....

....

....

....

....

....

....

....

....

....

....

Reread a familiar Bible passage and ask
God if there's anything new you can learn
that you have never noticed before.
Write your insights here!

....

....

....

....

....

....

....

....

....

....

....

....

....

I will give thanks to the Lord because He is right and good. I will sing praise to the name of the Lord Most High.

Psalm 7:17

What are you thankful for today?

Thank the Lord who gave those things (and much more!) to you.

....

....

....

....

....

....

....

....

....

....

....

Do you ever have doubts?
Or wonder about God's plan for you?

Read the verses below in your own Bible.
Highlight or underline the one that you feel
God is using to speak to your spirit. Jot down
anything you've learned from these verses to
help with your doubts and questions.

• Philippians 2:12–13   • 1 Corinthians 2:6–16
• Jeremiah 29:11–14

....

....

....

....

....

....

....

....

....

Is there anyone you need to forgive today?
Is there anyone you need to ask forgiveness from?

Make that effort. . .and write about it below:

How happy he is whose wrong-doing is forgiven,
and whose sin is covered! How happy is the man
whose sin the Lord does not hold against him,
and in whose spirit there is nothing false.

Psalm 32:1–2

....

....

....

....

....

....

....

....

....

....

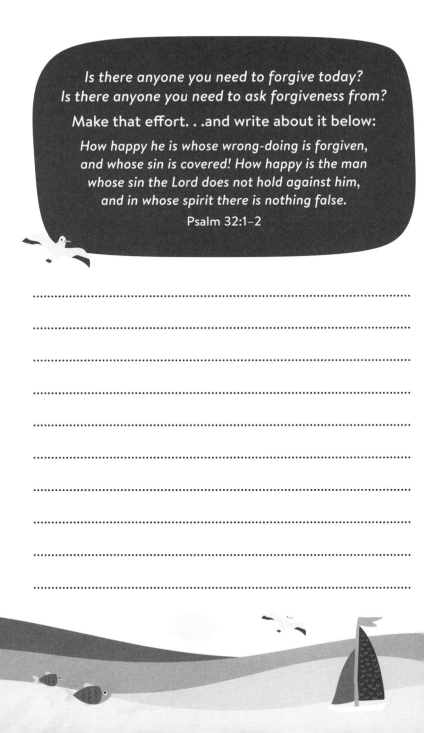

Look up Genesis 12:1–8.
Jot down the actions that Abraham
took in these verses.

What can you learn from Abraham's story?

....

....

....

....

....

....

....

....

....

....

....

....

....

Write your current prayer requests. Make sure to include today's date. As these prayers are answered, make sure that you note how and on what date. This will help to focus your heart on the ways God answers your prayers through His faithfulness. He doesn't always give you what you want, but He always supplies what you need.

Do not worry. Learn to pray about everything.
Give thanks to God as you ask Him for what you need.
Philippians 4:6

....

....

....

....

....

....

....

....

....

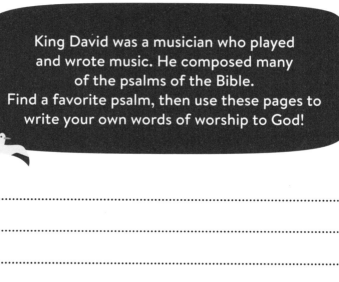

King David was a musician who played
and wrote music. He composed many
of the psalms of the Bible.
Find a favorite psalm, then use these pages to
write your own words of worship to God!

....

....

....

....

....

....

....

....

....

....

....

....

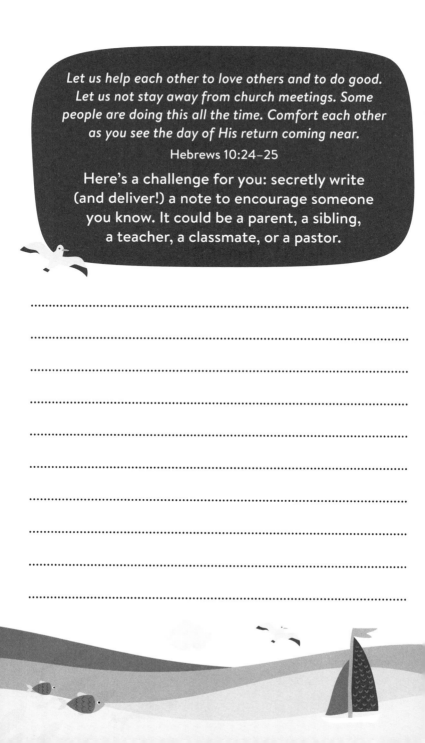

*Let us help each other to love others and to do good.
Let us not stay away from church meetings. Some
people are doing this all the time. Comfort each other
as you see the day of His return coming near.*
Hebrews 10:24–25

Here's a challenge for you: secretly write
(and deliver!) a note to encourage someone
you know. It could be a parent, a sibling,
a teacher, a classmate, or a pastor.

....

....

....

....

....

....

....

....

....

....

Read the book of Ruth—
it's only four short chapters!

*What do you learn about each of the major
characters: Ruth, Naomi, and Boaz?
How did God use Ruth in His big plans?*

....

....

....

....

....

....

....

....

....

....

....

....

God promises to keep all His promises. Look up the following verses, and write down some reasons you can believe what God says.

- Numbers 23:19
- Deuteronomy 7:9
- Psalm 89:34
- Isaiah 46:11
- Romans 4:21
- 2 Timothy 2:13
- Hebrews 6:18

....

....

....

....

....

....

....

....

....

....

Read Romans 12:6–8 to see what
God says about "spiritual gifts."

Do you know what your gift is?

Ask God to show you how to use
the gifts He's given you.

....

....

....

....

....

....

....

....

....

....

....

....

Choose a favorite Bible verse and dive deeper into it. First, write it out below, exactly as it is in your Bible. Then look up the same verse in other translations. (You can do this through Bible websites or apps, if you don't have other translations in your home.)

How do the differing words help you understand the verse?

....

....

....

....

....

....

....

....

....

Read the book of Jonah—
it's another short one!

*What do you learn about both
Jonah and the Ninevites?
How did God use Jonah in His big plans?*

....

....

....

....

....

....

....

....

....

....

....

....

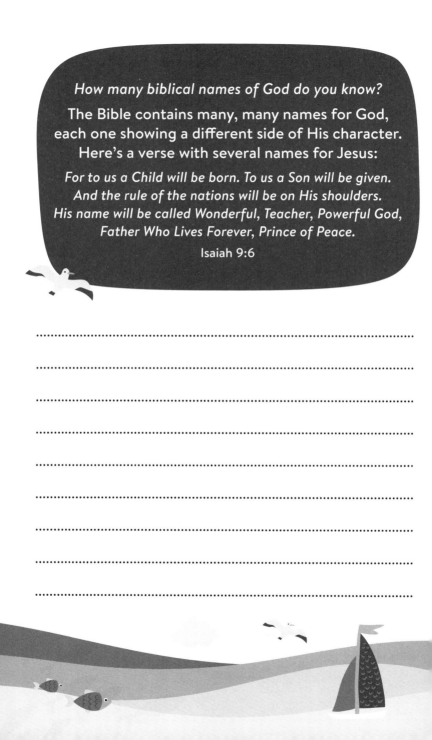

How many biblical names of God do you know?

The Bible contains many, many names for God, each one showing a different side of His character. Here's a verse with several names for Jesus:

For to us a Child will be born. To us a Son will be given. And the rule of the nations will be on His shoulders. His name will be called Wonderful, Teacher, Powerful God, Father Who Lives Forever, Prince of Peace.

Isaiah 9:6

....

....

....

....

....

....

....

....

....

Read John chapter 1.
Write down all the descriptions of Jesus.

Which one is most interesting to you?

....

....

....

....

....

....

....

....

....

....

....

....

....

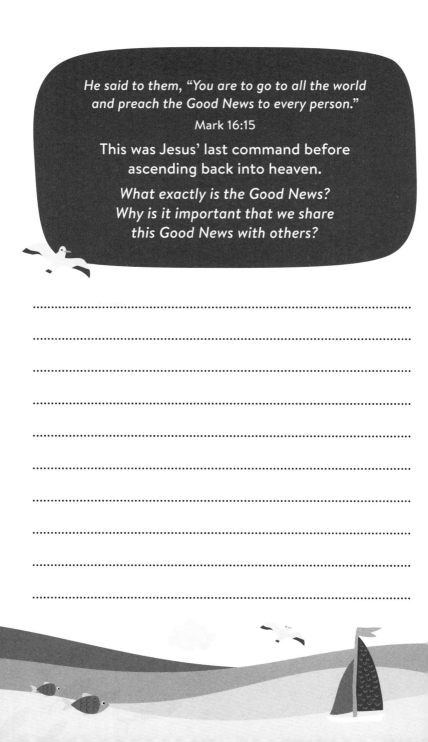

He said to them, "You are to go to all the world and preach the Good News to every person."

Mark 16:15

This was Jesus' last command before ascending back into heaven.

What exactly is the Good News? Why is it important that we share this Good News with others?

....

....

....

....

....

....

....

....

....

....

Skim through the Book of Esther,
and think about these questions:

- *Who are the main "characters" in the story?*
- *Where did the story take place?*
- *What happened in Esther that shows God's plan and purpose for His people?*
- *What can you learn from this story to help you live your own life?*

....

....

....

....

....

....

....

....

....

....

Find an important verse to
memorize, and write it below.
Now, memorize it!

....

....

....

....

....

....

....

....

....

....

....

....

....

Turn to Psalm 16.

What are some words the psalmist uses to describe how he feels in the God's presence? What are some words you would use to describe how you feel when you're with Him?

....

....

....

....

....

....

....

....

....

....

....

....

Ask a friend or family member about their favorite verse or passage of the Bible. Read that scripture in your own Bible and investigate it, making notes using the five Ws and an H we discussed earlier.

....

....

....

....

....

....

....

....

....

....

....

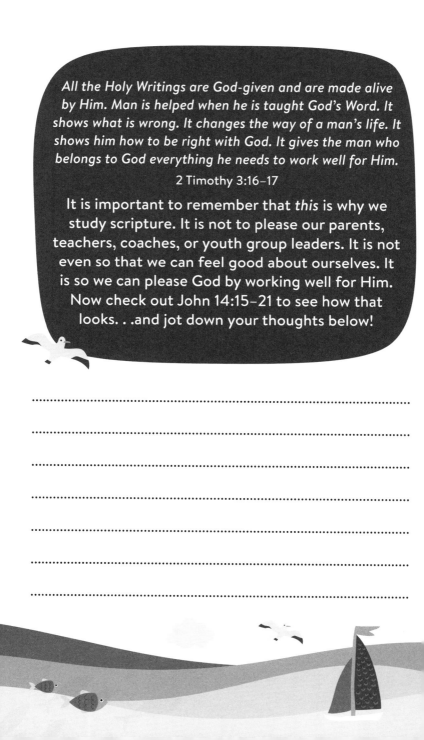

All the Holy Writings are God-given and are made alive by Him. Man is helped when he is taught God's Word. It shows what is wrong. It changes the way of a man's life. It shows him how to be right with God. It gives the man who belongs to God everything he needs to work well for Him.
2 Timothy 3:16–17

It is important to remember that *this* is why we study scripture. It is not to please our parents, teachers, coaches, or youth group leaders. It is not even so that we can feel good about ourselves. It is so we can please God by working well for Him. Now check out John 14:15–21 to see how that looks. . .and jot down your thoughts below!

Theology is the study of the nature of God. As you read the Bible, you are practicing the study of God's nature. When you learn something about His knowledge, or His power, or His character, or His love, write it down:

....

....

....

....

....

....

....

....

....

....

....

You know that the devil's a troublemaker.

What's the good news in these verses?

- Romans 16:20
- James 4:7
- 1 John 2:14; 5:18

....

....

....

....

....

....

....

....

....

....

....

....

Read John 10.

What do these verses tell us about Jesus' character?

....

....

....

....

....

....

....

....

....

....

....

....

Look up Ezra 7:10 and jot down answers
to the following questions:

• *What did Ezra do with his "heart"—his inner
desires—as it relates to God's Word? What
does that mean? Does this seem like a carefree
or a serious approach to Bible study?*

• *What are the three things Ezra wanted
to do with God's Word—also known as "the
Law of the Lord"? What are you hoping to
accomplish by your own Bible study?*

....

....

....

....

....

....

....

....

....

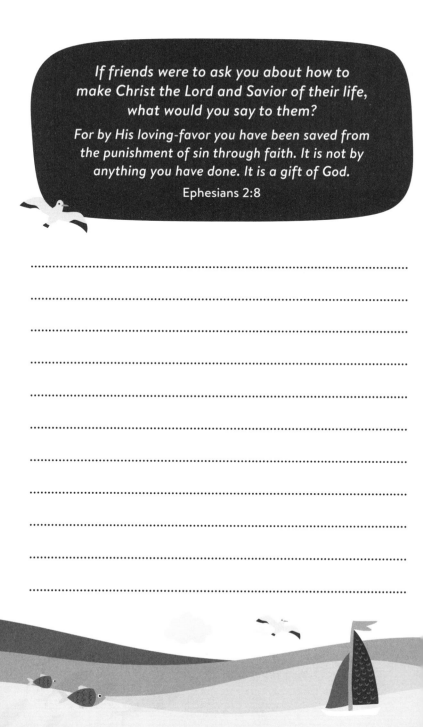

If friends were to ask you about how to make Christ the Lord and Savior of their life, what would you say to them?

For by His loving-favor you have been saved from the punishment of sin through faith. It is not by anything you have done. It is a gift of God.

Ephesians 2:8

....

....

....

....

....

....

....

....

....

....

....

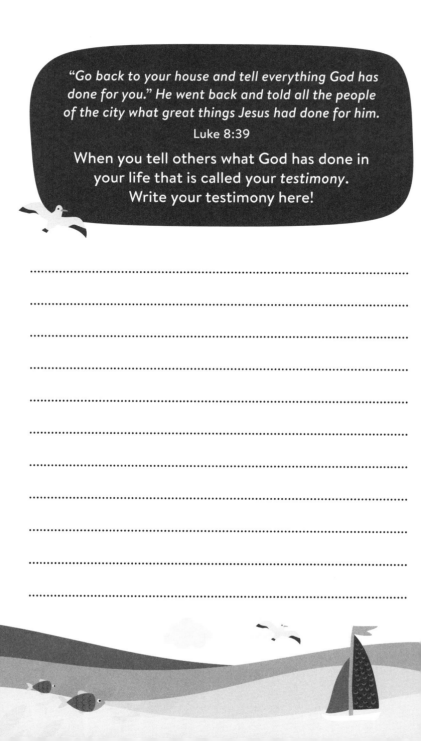

"Go back to your house and tell everything God has done for you." He went back and told all the people of the city what great things Jesus had done for him.

Luke 8:39

When you tell others what God has done in your life that is called your *testimony*.
Write your testimony here!

....

....

....

....

....

....

....

....

....

....

....

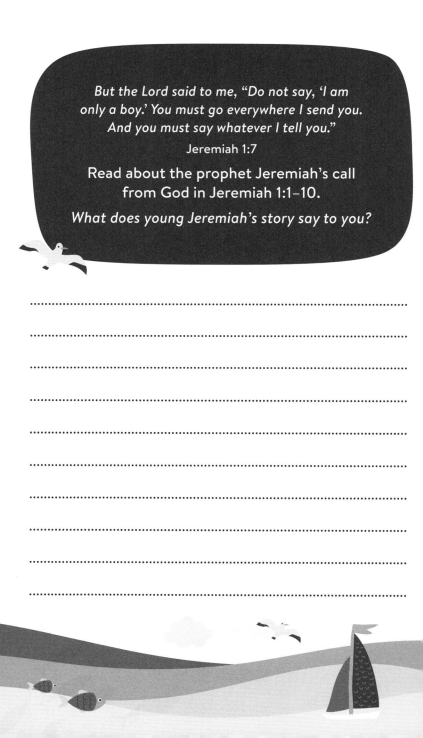

But the Lord said to me, "Do not say, 'I am only a boy.' You must go everywhere I send you. And you must say whatever I tell you."

Jeremiah 1:7

Read about the prophet Jeremiah's call from God in Jeremiah 1:1–10.

What does young Jeremiah's story say to you?

Look up Luke 24:45 and jot down answers
to the following questions:

• Look at the "context" of this verse—that is, the
verses that come before and after. What has recently
happened to Jesus? Who is He talking with now?

• In this verse, what does Jesus do for His followers
("disciples" in other translations of the Bible)?
What does that tell you about Bible study?

....

....

....

....

....

....

....

....

....

....

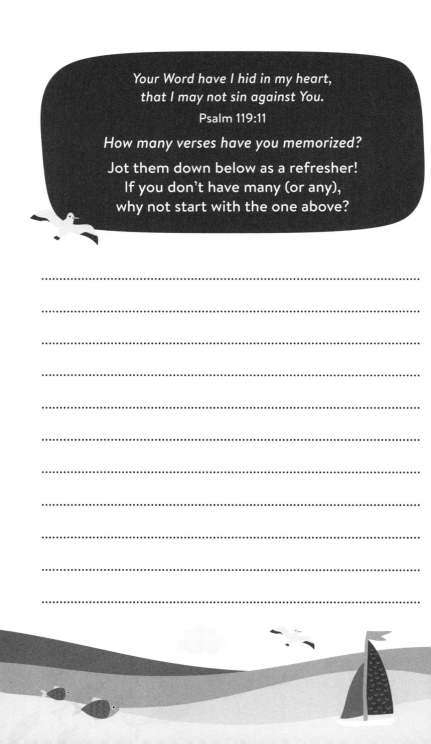

*Your Word have I hid in my heart,
that I may not sin against You.*

Psalm 119:11

How many verses have you memorized?

Jot them down below as a refresher!
If you don't have many (or any),
why not start with the one above?

....

....

....

....

....

....

....

....

....

....

....

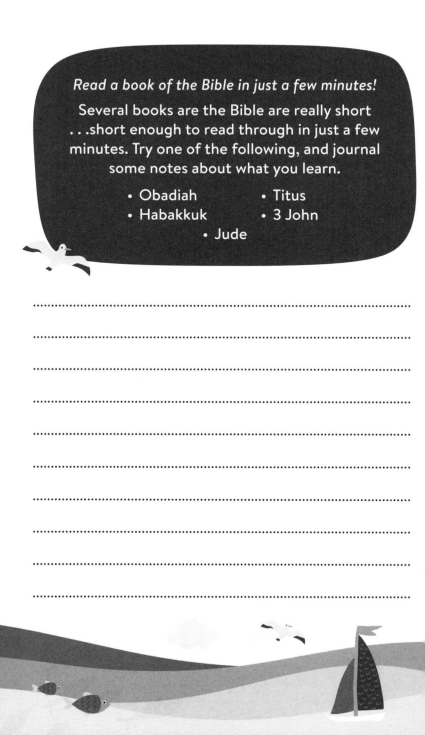

Read a book of the Bible in just a few minutes!

Several books are the Bible are really short
. . .short enough to read through in just a few
minutes. Try one of the following, and journal
some notes about what you learn.

- Obadiah
- Habakkuk
- Jude
- Titus
- 3 John

....

....

....

....

....

....

....

....

....

....

Is there a Bible character that you just don't understand? What did that person do that just doesn't make sense to you? Is there anything that person's life can still teach you?

....

....

....

....

....

....

....

....

....

....

....

....

....

Find three different verses that mention
the word *love.* Write them here.

What do you learn about love from these verses?

....

....

....

....

....

....

....

....

....

....

....

....

Look up Psalm 119:18 and answer the following questions:

- *What does the psalm writer want from God? How is this verse a prayer?*

- *What would you say to God before you begin your own Bible time?*

....

....

....

....

....

....

....

....

....

....

....

Get creative!

Using colored pencils, markers, or even letters cut from magazines, "dress up" a memory verse below. It's more than just art—your brain is using the creativity to better store the verse in your memory. Some good verses would include Psalm 119:105, Proverbs 3:5, Matthew 11:28, or 2 Corinthians 5:17.

....

....

....

....

....

....

....

....

....

....

Read 2 Timothy. . .it won't take long. The apostle Paul wrote this letter to his spiritual son, Timothy. Imagine that Paul was writing to *you*.

What would you learn from this letter?

....

....

....

....

....

....

....

....

....

....

....

....

....

Did you know that the Old Testament is divided into major sections?

It begins with five books of the Law, followed by twelve books of History, then five books of poetry, five books of the major prophets, and finally, twelve books of the minor prophets.

Write out the books of the Old Testament into these categories in the space below.

....

....

....

....

....

....

....

....

....

....

The New Testament has sections too!
The New Testament begins with the four Gospels,
followed by a history book, then twenty-one
letters, and finally a book of prophecy.

Categorize the twenty-seven books
of the New Testament below.

....

....

....

....

....

....

....

....

....

....

....

Check out the Old Testament book of Judges.
Write down the names of the judges of Israel,
and something about each one.

....

....

....

....

....

....

....

....

....

....

....

....

....

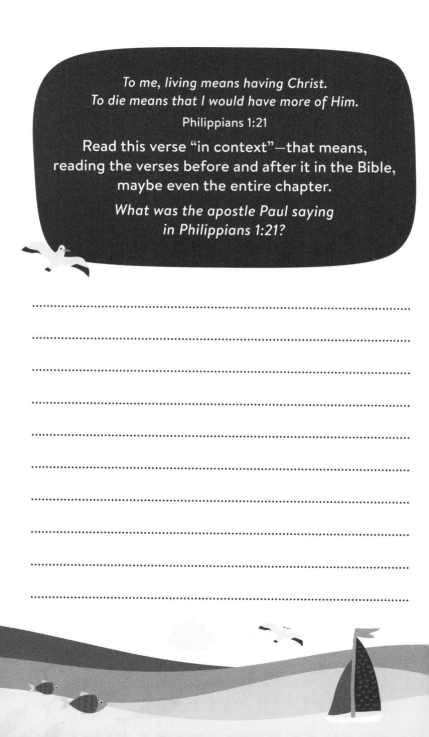

*To me, living means having Christ.
To die means that I would have more of Him.*

Philippians 1:21

Read this verse "in context"—that means,
reading the verses before and after it in the Bible,
maybe even the entire chapter.

*What was the apostle Paul saying
in Philippians 1:21?*

....

....

....

....

....

....

....

....

....

....

Read and consider these great verses describing the abundant (or full) life that Jesus offers:

- John 10:10, 14:19
- Romans 6:8, 11
- Ephesians 2:1, 5–6
- 1 John 5:12

....

....

....

....

....

....

....

....

....

....

....

....

....

Read Ecclesiastes 3:1–8.

• *What word is repeated numerous times in this passage? What does the author seem to be saying?*

....

....

....

....

....

....

....

....

....

....

....

....

An important reminder: Bible knowledge is only as good as the actions that follow. So *do what the Bible says*, whatever you're learning in your study.

....

....

....

....

....

....

....

....

....

....

....

....

....

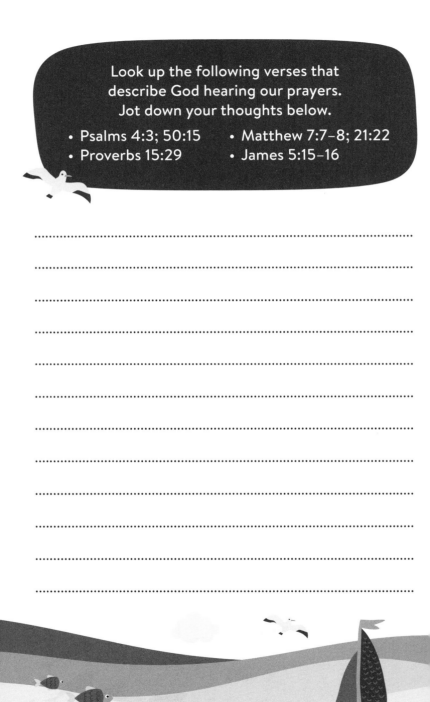

Look up the following verses that
describe God hearing our prayers.
Jot down your thoughts below.

• Psalms 4:3; 50:15
• Proverbs 15:29
• Matthew 7:7–8; 21:22
• James 5:15–16

....
....
....
....
....
....
....
....
....
....
....
....

Check out Revelation 4:1–11.

What do you learn about heaven from these verses?

....

....

....

....

....

....

....

....

....

....

....

....

....

Be glad you can do the things you should be doing.
Do all things without arguing and talking about
how you wish you did not have to do them. In
that way, you can prove yourselves to be without
blame. You are God's children and no one can
talk against you, even in a sin-loving and sin-sick
world. You are to shine as lights among the sinful
people of this world. Take a strong hold on the
Word of Life. Then when Christ comes again, I will
be happy that I did not work with you for nothing.

Philippians 2:14–16

Are there any duties in life you find hard
to enjoy? Chores? Homework? The Bible
says we can be glad when we do hard things,
if we do them for God's glory.
What instruction do these verses give you?

....

....

....

....

....

....

Here are some verses that offer help
in overcoming temptation.

What are the main points from each one?

- Romans 8:37
- 1 Corinthians 10:13
- 2 Corinthians 12:9

- Hebrews 2:18
- 2 Peter 2:9
- 1 John 4:4

....

....

....

....

....

....

....

....

....

....

....

Let's go back to the very beginning. Look up Genesis 1 and write out what was made on each day of creation.

Why do you think God made things in the order He did?

....

....

....

....

....

....

....

....

....

....

....

....

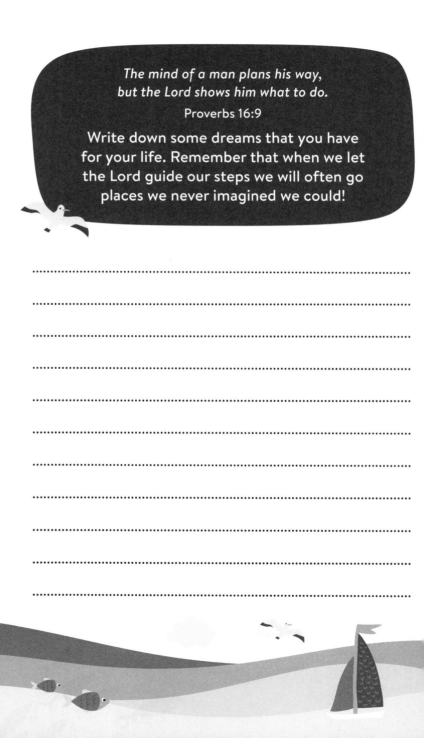

The mind of a man plans his way,
but the Lord shows him what to do.

Proverbs 16:9

Write down some dreams that you have
for your life. Remember that when we let
the Lord guide our steps we will often go
places we never imagined we could!

....

....

....

....

....

....

....

....

....

....

Everyone gets lonely at times.
*But what do these verses say about
the person who seeks God?*

- 1 Chronicles 28:9
- 2 Chronicles 15:2
- Psalm 9:10
- Jeremiah 29:13
- Amos 5:4
- Acts 17:27
- Hebrews 11:6

....

....

....

....

....

....

....

....

....

....

....

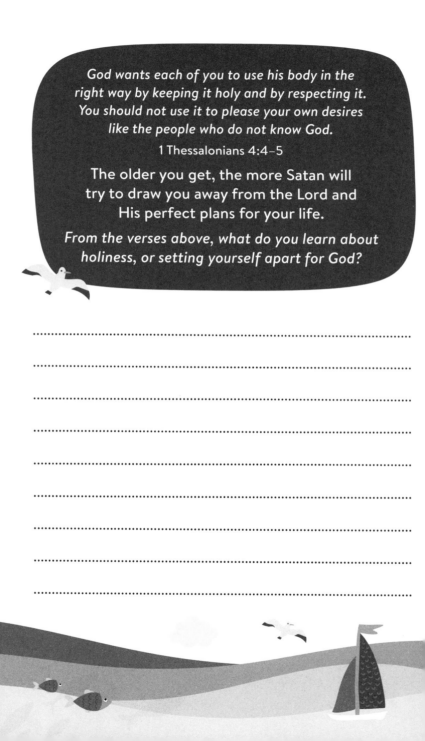

God wants each of you to use his body in the right way by keeping it holy and by respecting it. You should not use it to please your own desires like the people who do not know God.

1 Thessalonians 4:4–5

The older you get, the more Satan will try to draw you away from the Lord and His perfect plans for your life.

From the verses above, what do you learn about holiness, or setting yourself apart for God?

....

....

....

....

....

....

....

....

....

Matthew 5:1–12 is a section of scripture called "the Beatitudes."

What words or phrases appear over and over in this passage? Which of Jesus' words describe your life the best?

....

....

....

....

....

....

....

....

....

....

....

....

The New Testament books of Matthew, Mark, and Luke are called the "synoptic Gospels" because they are "seen together," the meaning of *synoptic*. When you read the same story in the synoptic Gospels, you get the full picture.

Try reading the story of the feeding of the five thousand from each of these Gospels.

What is the same? What is different? What do you learn from reading the different perspectives?

- Matthew 14:13–21
- Mark 6:30–44
- Luke 9:10–17

....

....

....

....

....

....

....

....

Matthew, Mark, Luke, and John are called "the Gospels," and there's also the "Gospel of Jesus Christ". . .the word *Gospel* means "good news."

What is that?

Read 1 Corinthians 15:1–11 to find out!

....

....

....

....

....

....

....

....

....

....

....

....

Look up Proverbs 17:17 and John 15:13, and jot down what these verses teach about friendship.

....

....

....

....

....

....

....

....

....

....

....

....

....

Here are some Bible characters, both famous and less well known, all worth knowing. Use a concordance or an online/app search to find their stories. . .and consider the five Ws and an H questions:

- Abel
- Barnabas
- Cornelius
- Daniel

- Miriam
- Nicodemus
- Rahab
- Samson

....

....

....

....

....

....

....

....

....

....

Confession—or admitting our sin to God—
is an important part of our relationship
with God and others. See what these
verses have to say about it:

- 1 John 1:9   • James 5:16
               • Psalm 51

....

....

....

....

....

....

....

....

....

....

....

> What can we learn about Jesus Christ
> from Philippians 2:5–11?

....

....

....

....

....

....

....

....

....

....

....

....

....

....

Have you ever heard someone say that there are many roads to heaven? How would you answer someone who said that to you? Here are some verses to get you thinking:

- John 14:6
- 1 Timothy 2:5
- Acts 4:12, 16:30–31

....

....

....

....

....

....

....

....

....

....

....

You know that Jesus was born as a baby on the first Christmas, then lived and died as a man on earth. But how does he appear now, in heaven?

Jot down (or try to draw!) details from Revelation 1:12–20.

....

....

....

....

....

....

....

....

....

....

....

....

Psalm 117 is the shortest chapter in the Bible. . .just two verses!

What is the theme of Psalm 117, from the opening and closing words? How is God described in this brief psalm?

....

....

....

....

....

....

....

....

....

....

....

....

Psalm 119 is the longest chapter in the Bible.

*Look through its 176 verses. . .
what is the overall theme?
In this psalm, what are the many
names for God's Word?*

....

....

....

....

....

....

....

....

....

....

....

....

Tips for memorizing scripture:

1. Choose a verse or passage that speaks to a need in your life.
2. Write the words and put them in a prominent place: on your bathroom mirror, bedroom door, or school locker.
3. Get a friend to memorize with you and quiz each other.

What passage are you memorizing right now?

....

....

....

....

....

....

....

....

....

What do the following scriptures tell Christians about the way they should live in this world?

- Romans 12:2
- John 15:19
- 1 John 2:15–17

....

....

....

....

....

....

....

....

....

....

....

....

....

Psalm 103 is a song of praise
to God written by David.
List the things that David praises God for.

....

....

....

....

....

....

....

....

....

....

....

....

....

If you could make a movie out of any Bible story, which would it be?

Describe how the movie would play out.

....

....

....

....

....

....

....

....

....

....

....

....

When you believe in Jesus, He gives you eternal life. Look up the following verses and write some details about that life that lasts forever.

- John 14:2–3
- Romans 2:7
- 1 Corinthians 2:9
- Hebrews 4:9
- 1 Peter 1:9
- 2 Peter 3:13
- Revelation 3:4

....

....

....

....

....

....

....

....

....

....

What does Mark 12:41–44 teach about giving?

....

....

....

....

....

....

....

....

....

....

....

....

....

....

Deuteronomy 6:4–9 is a prayer that the Jewish people say every morning and evening. Jesus would have learned this prayer as a young boy and would have recited it twice a day throughout His life.

Write it below, and underline all the verbs (the action words) directed toward you.

....

....

....

....

....

....

....

....

....

....

Here are some verses that promise
victory over the world.

What can you learn from each?

- John 16:33, 17:15   • Galatians 1:4; 6:14
  • 1 John 5:4–5

....

....

....

....

....

....

....

....

....

....

....

....

James is an easy-to-understand book when you want guidance on the Christian life. Choose a chapter to read, and jot down what it tells you to do. Then do those things!

....

....

....

....

....

....

....

....

....

....

....

....

....

Children, as Christians, obey your parents. This is the right thing to do. Respect your father and mother. This is the first Law given that had a promise. The promise is this: If you respect your father and mother, you will live a long time and your life will be full of many good things.

Ephesians 6:1–3

As we get older, it can become harder to obey and respect parents. . .but God commands it. Write down some of your challenges with your parents, and consider ways of honoring both them and God, who gave them to you.

....

....

....

....

....

....

....

....

If you could have dinner with any Bible character, who would it be? Why?

....

....

....

....

....

....

....

....

....

....

....

....

....

....

Look up these verses about Jesus' return to earth.

What "facts and figures" stand out to you?

- Matthew 24:30
- Mark 14:62
- John 14:3
- 1 Thessalonians 4:16–17
- 1 Corinthians 4:5
- 2 Timothy 4:8
- Revelation 1:7

....

....

....

....

....

....

....

....

....

....

....

Find three different verses that mention the word *peace*. Write them below.

What do these verses teach about peace?

....

....

....

....

....

....

....

....

....

....

....

....

....

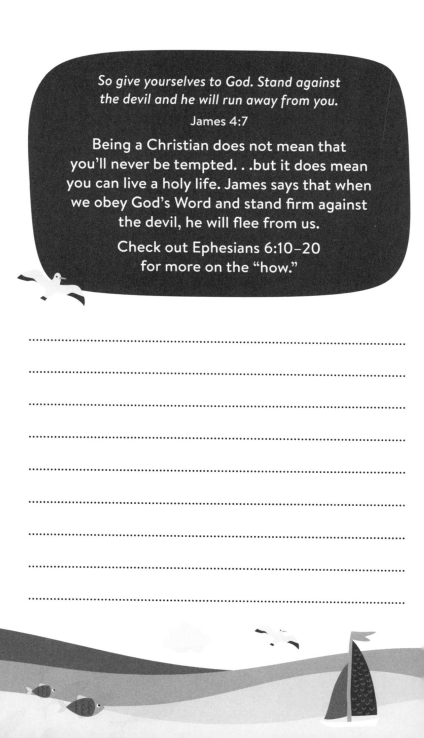

So give yourselves to God. Stand against the devil and he will run away from you.

James 4:7

Being a Christian does not mean that you'll never be tempted. . .but it does mean you can live a holy life. James says that when we obey God's Word and stand firm against the devil, he will flee from us.

Check out Ephesians 6:10–20 for more on the "how."

*Ever felt like no one in the world
truly understands you?*

God understands and loves you completely.

*Check out Psalm 139. . .what are some things
that He knows about you?*

....

....

....

....

....

....

....

....

....

....

....

....

Who is praying for you each day? Maybe a parent or grandparent, a friend or a teacher? What do the following verses say?

• Romans 8:34   • Hebrews 7:25

....

....

....

....

....

....

....

....

....

....

....

....

Find an important verse to memorize,
and write it below.

Now, memorize it!

....

....

....

....

....

....

....

....

....

....

....

....

....

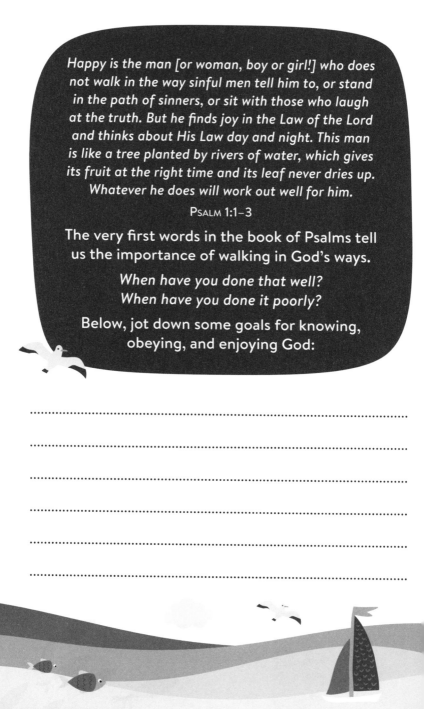

Happy is the man [or woman, boy or girl!] who does not walk in the way sinful men tell him to, or stand in the path of sinners, or sit with those who laugh at the truth. But he finds joy in the Law of the Lord and thinks about His Law day and night. This man is like a tree planted by rivers of water, which gives its fruit at the right time and its leaf never dries up. Whatever he does will work out well for him.

PSALM 1:1–3

The very first words in the book of Psalms tell us the importance of walking in God's ways.

When have you done that well?
When have you done it poorly?

Below, jot down some goals for knowing, obeying, and enjoying God:

....

....

....

....

....

....

ALSO FROM DIVE IN!

Want to know God better? Then learn to study His Word! The *Dive In! Kids' Study Bible* will guide you into a lifelong adventure of learning, through the easy-to-understand New Life™ Version text and 36 colorful inserts that explain the why's and how's of going deep into scripture yourself.

Hardback / 978-1-64352-292-0 / $24.99